AF415127

SPIRITUAL NOBILITY

The Story of Joseph

LEADING GOD'S PEOPLE
BOOK 13

ZACHARIAS TANEE FOMUM

Copyright © 1985 by Zacharias Tanee Fomum
All rights reserved.

No part of this book may be reproduced in any form or by any electronic or
mechanical means, including information storage and retrieval systems,
without written permission from the author, except for the use of brief
quotations in a book review.

The version of the Bible used in this book is the *Revised Standard Version*,
except stated otherwise.

Published by

*A division of the Book Ministry of Christian
Missionary Fellowship International*

info@books4revival.com

CONTENTS

PREFACE

Spiritual Nobility—the story of Joseph, is a book written in 1985 by Professor Zacharias Tanee Fomum. In this book, the author presents Joseph in the school of the wilderness (sold as a slave, then became a prisoner). God is jealous of all special vessels who are in His training school. He will not allow them to be independent. It is of utmost importance to Him. He did not spare His own Son, the Lord Jesus Christ, who underwent a crash course of 40 days in the wilderness, because He knew that those who have experienced great periods of trials know how to handle greatness. He equally gives us the secret of Joseph's greatness which is summarised in this Bible passage:

"The Lord was with Joseph."

Through this book, the author wants to help you handle without grumbling the wilderness" you are going through or may go through, because you are a special vessel God wants to use.

Dear reader, you are in good company. We pray that the Lord would use this book to make of you a person who depends totally on God for that is the secret of greatness according to God. It is the secret of SPIRITUAL NOBILITY.

INTRODUCTION

THE GENESIS OF THE PROBLEM

Jacob dwelt in the land of his father's sojournings, in the land of Canaan. This is the history of the family of Jacob. Joseph, being seventeen years old, was shepherding the flock with his brothers; he was a lad with the sons of Bilhah and Zilpah, his father's wives; and Joseph brought an ill report of them to their father. Now Israel loved Joseph more than any other of his children, because he was the son of his old age; and he made him a long robe with sleeves. But when his brothers saw that their father loved him more than all his brothers, they hated him, and could not speak peaceably to him.

Now Joseph had a dream, and when he told it to his brothers they only hated him the more. He said to them, "Hear this dream which I have dreamed: behold, we were binding sheaves in the field, and lo, my sheaf arose and stood upright; and behold, your sheaves gathered round it, and bowed down to my sheaf." His brothers said to him, "Are you indeed to reign over us? Or are you indeed to have dominion over us?" So they hated him yet more for his dreams and for his words. Then he dreamed another dream, and told it to his brothers, and said, "Behold, I have dreamed another dream; and behold, the sun, the moon, and eleven stars were bowing down to me." But when he told it to his father and to his brothers, his father rebuked him, and said to him, "What is this dream that you have dreamed? Shall I and your mother and your brothers indeed come to bow ourselves to the ground before you?" And his brothers were jealous of him, but his father kept the saying in mind" (Genesis 37:1–11).

God had a special purpose for Joseph. When the account of his life story begins, it is as a young boy of seventeen that we meet him. He was not an idle youth, but hardworking. The Bible says:

Joseph being seventeen years old was shepherding the flock with his brothers (Genesis 37:2).

That is a wonderful place to begin, not with a lazy youth but a young man committed to hard work.

Four things combined made life a serious problem for Joseph.

First of all, he took upon himself the necessary but unpopular ministry of exposing the sin of his brothers. The Bible says:

And Joseph brought an ill-report of them to their father (Genesis 37: 2).

Joseph broke the rule of safety. No one who wants to be safe should expose sin. He committed a crime against an easy-going society! We live in a day that is destitute of true courage. From the pulpit the prophets of false peace tell a sin-ridden world that God is about to pour His mightiest blessings on an unrepentant humanity. Such prophets want to be safe. They want to be accepted, courted and petted. May God deliver me from being caught in such a snare. Joseph was different. He was interested in the glory of God and that glory alone. He had abandoned all desires to be safe. May God raise such men in this nation, true prophets of the unpopular!

Joseph did not only expose sin; he was loved by his father.

> *Now Israel loved Joseph more than any other of his children because he was the son of his old age; and he made him a long robe with sleeves* (Genesis 37:3).

Joseph was loved by his father and this created jealousy from his brothers. We insist that all who would earn the father's love would be persecuted. The flesh cannot allow others to be preferred! The sad thing is that even in a local church that has known the power of the Lord, there will be only a few who would go the whole way and see their flesh crucified. May God deliver His servants from such terrible sin.

Had Joseph only exposed sin and won his father's heart, things wouldn't have been so bad for him. The problem is that he added to his unpopularity by being a special recipient of divine revelation.

JOSEPH'S DREAMS—THE INDISPENSABLE REVELATION

God spoke to Joseph by dreams. The Bible says,

> *Now Joseph had a dream, and when he told it to his brothers they only hated him the more. He said to them, "Hear this dream which I have dreamed: behold, we were binding sheaves in the field, and lo, my sheaf arose and stood upright; and behold, your sheaves gathered round it, and bowed down to my sheaf"* (Genesis 37:5–6).

This was no ordinary dream; it was a revelation of what was to come. Joseph did not give himself that position of greatness; it must even have surprised him that God was going to thus exalt him.

This revelation did not bring joy to the others. It only gave them grounds to hate him the more. The Bible says that,

They only hated him the more (Genesis 37:5).

Was it his fault that God had chosen him for honour? His brothers did not only hate him they took him to task with questions.

...Are you indeed to reign over us? Or are you indeed to have dominion over us?... (Genesis 37:8).

These are indeed difficult questions to answer. How could Joseph answer them? He was not the author of the revelation. How could he defend it? He received it from the Lord and his sole duty was to say that God had so said. Being unable to explain it, he must have appeared to them as very proud and arrogant and this only intensified their hatred. The Bible says,

So they hated him more for his dreams and for his words (Genesis 37:8).

There will always be some hatred for exposing sin. There will always be some hatred for standing in a privileged position and being loved by the Lord. However, this is nothing compared to the hatred for the one who has received revelation. Why is that so? I believe it is because a special revelation sets a man apart for God's use in a very special way. From that point on, the man is lost to the world, lost to the flesh, lost to the devil as never before. A man with a revelation is a man apart. From that time on, others may not understand him anymore. How could such a life not invoke hatred from his brothers for Joseph? If we have received a special revelation and are not hated, it must be because we are compromising somewhere.

God always reinforces every revelation that He gives to His distinctive servants. He never speaks just once. He reveals a thing once and then again to further establish, strengthen and broaden what He had earlier said. He said to Paul,

> *...I have appeared to you for this purpose, to appoint you to serve and bear witness to the things in which you have seen me and to those which I will appear to you* (Acts 26:16). So with Joseph, the revelation was made a second time. The Bible says, *Then he dreamed another dream, and told it to his brothers, and said, "Behold I have dreamed another dream; and behold the sun, the moon, and the eleven stars were bowing down to me"* (Genesis 37:9).

The Lord had extended the reign of his authority and power; his parents were to join the rank of those that bowed to him.

This earned him a rebuke. Even his father who loved him so well rebuked him. Revelation will set us apart and cause problems between us and the people who love us most dearly. Was it not for this reason that Jesus the Lord of glory said,

> *Do not think that I have come to bring peace on earth; I have not come to bring peace but a sword. For I have come to set a man against his father, and a daughter against her mother, and a daughter-in-law against her mother-in-law; and a man's foes will be those of his own household. He who loves father or mother more than me is not worthy of me; and he who loves son or daughter more than me*

is not worthy of me; and he who does not take his cross and follow me is not worthy of me (Matthew 10:34–38).

The Body of Christ languishes for lack of people with a clear revelation from the Lord. I encourage you to seek the Lord and receive from Him that unique and far-reaching revelation. However, I want you to be sure that you will be hated for it.

THE PRICE OF RIGHTEOUSNESS—1

They saw him afar off, and before he came near to them they conspired against him to kill him. They said to one another, "Here comes this dreamer.

Come now, let us kill him and throw him into one of the pits; then we shall say that a wild beast has devoured him, and we shall see what will become of his dreams." But when Reuben heard it, he delivered him out of their hands, saying, "Let us not take his life." And Reuben said to them, "Shed no blood; cast him into this pit here in the wilderness, but lay no hand upon him"—that he might rescue him out of their hand, to restore him to his father.

So when Joseph came to his brothers, they stripped him of his robe, the long robe with sleeves that he wore; and they took him and cast him into a pit. The pit was empty, there was no water in it.

Then they sat down to eat; and looking up they saw a caravan of Ish'maelites coming from Gilead, with their camels bearing gum, balm, and myrrh, on their way to carry it down to Egypt.

Then Judah said to his brothers, "What profit is it if we slay our brother and conceal his blood? Come, let us sell him to the Ish'-

maelites, and let not our hand be upon him, for he is our brother, our own flesh." And his brothers heeded him.

Then Mid'ianite traders passed by; and they drew Joseph up and lifted him out of the pit, and sold him to the Ish'maelites for twenty shekels of silver; and they took Joseph to Egypt.

When Reuben returned to the pit and saw that Joseph was not in the pit, he rent his clothes and returned to his brothers, and said, "The lad is gone; and I, where shall I go?" Then they took Joseph's robe, and killed a goat, and dipped the robe in the blood; and they sent the long robe with sleeves and brought it to their father, and said, "This we have found; see now whether it is your son's robe or not." And he recognized it, and said, "It is my son's robe; a wild beast has devoured him; Joseph is without doubt torn to pieces." Then Jacob rent his garments, and put sackcloth upon his loins, and mourned for his son many days. All his sons and all his daughters rose up to comfort him; but he refused to be comforted, and said, "No, I shall go down to Sheol to my son, mourning." Thus his father wept for him. Meanwhile the Mid'ianites had sold him in Egypt to Pot'i-phar, an officer of Pharaoh, the captain of the guard (Genesis 37:18–36).

1. THE SINFULNESS OF SIN

Jealousy, if not gotten rid of, will mature and produce death. Had Joseph's brethren repented of their jealousy, the story would have been different. The tragedy is that they did not repent.

Then desire when it has conceived gives birth to sin; and sin when it is full-grown brings forth death (James 1:15). They worked out an evil plan, ...*Here comes this dreamer* (Genesis 37:19).

It was not "Behold our brother comes" but "this dreamer". He acquired a nickname because of his special relationship with the Lord.

One sin often leads to another, for no sin can be committed in isolation. Firstly, they decided to kill him (murder). Secondly, they decided to kill a young goat in order to use its blood to cover their sin (waste). Thirdly, they pretended that they did not know to whom the coat belonged (pretence). Fourthly, they said, "This we have found; see now whether it is your son's robe or not" (lying). Fifthly, they sold him. Sixthly, they caused their father endless heartache.

Dear reader, are you on the pathway to commit some sin? I beg you, do not go that way. It will lead to many things far more horrible than you ever dreamt you would be in. Sin will always produce more sin. King David just committed the sin of idleness. But this sin led to adultery, then to causing Uriah to be drunk, then to murder, etc. I beg you, please, withdraw from the way of sin, even the smallest sin.

2. THE IMPOTENCY OF COMPROMISE: A PILATE WITHOUT COURAGE

Reuben stands in the story we are treating as a kind of Pilate —a man without courage. He did not want Joseph dead. In fact, he did not seem to join his brothers in their hatred for him. He was anxious to have him released. He had authority. He was the eldest son. He could just have said, "This is nonsense. Let us stop it," and the plot would have ended. However, he was a man without moral courage. He danced to the tune of the majority. He said,

"Let us not take his life." "Shed no blood; cast him into this pit here in the wilderness, but lay no hand upon him..." (Genesis 37:21;22);

that he might rescue him out of their hands, to restore him to their father. He wanted to win both worlds. Many believers are like that. They want heaven but they are infatuated with the world. They are divided at heart. Apostle James says,

Unfaithful creatures! Do you not know that friendship with the world is enmity with God? Therefore whoever wishes to be a friend of the world makes himself an enemy of God (James 4:4).

Compromise often leads to heartbreak. Reuben later discovered that Joseph was no longer in the pit and he rent his clothes and cried (Genesis 37:29,30). Compromise never accomplishes anything solid. Reuben failed hopelessly in his attempts to save Joseph by the way of compromise. What the Lord needs today is men and women of courage who will stand for the truth at any cost. Today, religious negotiators have replaced prophets in the leadership of the churches. May God raise prophets! May He put aside compromisers!!

3. INTO EGYPT

Can you imagine the sorrow and loneliness of Joseph? He was just seventeen, yet, he is now treated as some merchandise. His brothers sold him to the Midianites and they took him into Egypt. He was not only a slave. He was a lonely slave far from home—in Egypt. What was his crime? Revelation! Vision!!

2

THE PRICE OF RIGHTEOUSNESS—2

Now Joseph was taken down to Egypt, and Pot'i-phar, an officer of Pharaoh, the captain of the guard, an Egyptian, bought him from the Ish'maelites who had brought him down there. The LORD was with Joseph, and he became a successful man; and he was in the house of his master the Egyptian, and his master saw that the LORD was with him, and that the LORD caused all that he did to prosper in his hands. So Joseph found favor in his sight and attended him, and he made him overseer of his house and put him in charge of all that he had. From the time that he made him overseer in his house and over all that he had the LORD blessed the Egyptian's house for Joseph's sake; the blessing of the LORD was upon all that he had, in house and field. So he left all that he had in Joseph's charge; and having him he had no concern for anything but the food which he ate.

Now Joseph was handsome and good-looking. And after a time his master's wife cast her eyes upon Joseph, and said, "Lie with me." But he refused and said to his master's wife, "Lo, having me my master has no concern about anything in the house, and he has put everything that he has in my hand; he is not greater in this house than I am; nor has he kept back anything from me except yourself, because you are his wife; how then can I do this great wickedness, and sin against God?" And although she spoke to Joseph day after day, he would not listen to her, to lie with her or to be with her. But one day, when he went into the house to do his work and none of the men of the house was there in the house, she caught him by his garment, saying, "Lie with me." But he left his garment in her hand, and fled and got out of the house. And when she saw that he had left his garment in her hand, and had fled out of the house, she called to the men of her household and said to them, "See, he has brought among us a Hebrew to insult us; he came in to me to lie with me, and I cried out with a loud voice; and when he heard that I lifted up my voice and cried, he left his garment with me, and fled and got out of the house." Then she laid up his garment by her until his master came home, and she told him the same story, saying, "The Hebrew servant, whom you have brought among us, came in to me to insult me; but as soon as I lifted up my voice and cried, he left his garment with me, and fled out of the house."

When his master heard the words which his wife spoke to him , "This is the way your servant treated me," his anger was kindled. And Joseph's master took him and put him into the prison, the place where the king's prisoners were confined, and he was there in prison. But the LORD was with Joseph and showed him steadfast love, and gave him favor in the sight of the keeper of the prison. And the keeper of the prison committed to Joseph's care all the prisoners who were in the prison; and whatever was done there, he was the doer of it; the keeper of the prison paid no heed to anything that was in Joseph's care, because the LORD was with him; and whatever he did, the LORD made it prosper (Genesis 39:1–23)

1. JOSEPH'S PROSPERITY

*I*n Egypt, Joseph was again sold. However, though far from home, the Lord was with him, and made him successful. His master soon saw the mark of God upon him. The Lord caused all that Joseph did to prosper. What a God! What we need is not the companionship of family or the companionship of the crowd. We need the companionship of the Lord and that is enough. God is recruiting an army of valiant soldiers for Himself. They are mainly lonely people; separated from the world, separated from the bulk and mass of easy-going Christianity; separated unto God. With such there is no limit to what He can do.

Joseph found favour in the sight of Potiphar. This was positive favour. This favour made Potiphar appoint him overseer of his house and put him in charge of all that he had, (Genesis 39:4). Joseph was thus promoted. With this promotion came added blessings for Potiphar. The Bible says,

> *From the time that he made him overseer in his house and over all that he had the LORD blessed the Egyptian's house for Joseph's sake; the blessing of the LORD was upon all that he had, in house and field* (Genesis 39:5).

We too are to be instruments of blessing to the world. We need to stop and ask ourselves, "Is the world richer because of my presence or does my presence make it poorer?"

If our presence only brings judgement to the world, then something is deficient in our walk with God. The presence of the Lord Jesus brought blessings to the world—diseases disappeared and hunger was stopped. May we be like Him—instruments of blessings. May the world be a poorer place when we pass out of it into the glory of our heavenly Father because of the gap that our departure would cause.

As Joseph brought blessings, so he rose in rank. The Bible says of Potiphar,

> *So he left all that he had in Joseph's charge; and having him he had no concern for anything but the food which he ate* (Genesis 39:6).

What a privileged position to be in and what great responsibilities go with it. Can you be trusted with so much? Are you faithful in the little that God has placed under your charge? Joseph was faithful. Glory be to the Lord. May He raise in the church many of the same calibre.

2. TEMPTATION AND VICTORY

Joseph was handsome and good looking. There is nothing wrong with this. His master had been drawn to him because of the touch of God on his life. He found positive favour with him. Now his master's wife was drawn to him not because of the Lord's touch on his life but because of his good looks. This was negative favour. She

> *"cast her eyes upon Joseph"* (Genesis 39:7).

Here were eyes of disastrous greed bent on fleshly satisfaction at all costs. She looked at him and all at once she wanted to possess him. She was not satisfied to let her lustful passions burn in her dirty heart. She actually vomited them out, "Lie with me," she said. How terrible! She was the mistress of the house and he was the slave-servant; yet she could initiate such condescending evil.

Praise the Lord for the man that Joseph was. He was a man after God's own heart. He turned her down. He did not only refuse quietly and politely as some of us out of carnal pity and politeness are tempted to do. He gave her a good lecture, a sermon. Listen to the sermon,

> *...Lo, having me my master has not concern about anything in the house, and he has put everything that he has in my hand; he is not greater in this house than I am; nor he has kept back anything from me, except yourself, because you are his wife; how then can I do this great wickedness, and sin against God?* (Genesis 39:9).

Joseph recognised the limits of his authority in the house. It extended over everything in the house except over her body. May the Lord help us to know the limits of our freedom with people. May He enable us to know the limits of what we may say and when we must not speak a word. When He shows us our limits, may we receive grace from Him not to exceed them even for one second and even by one centimetre. This is of utmost importance. No one who wants to go far with God dares ignore this.

Joseph said to her, "How then can I do this wickedness and sin against God?"

Joseph saw sin for what it actually is. Sin is not only transgression of the law. It is not only error; it is not only a mistake. It is great wickedness. Every sin deliberately undertaken is great wickedness. It is re-crucifying Christ; it is the stabbing of the righteous heart of God. That is what every sin is. My dear Saint, even the smallest lie, slander, gossip that issues from your lips is great wickedness.

Joseph did not only know that sin is great wickedness. He knew that it is wickedness against God. All sin is against God. When David fell into sin he put it rightly:

> *Against thee, thee only, have I sinned, and done that which is evil in thy sight...* (Psalm 51:4).

Joseph preached to her but the sermon did not put her off. She was so committed to having her way that she did not truly listen. She continued to press her point day by day. Many who overcame the first and second time would have yielded at this persistence. All of hell was bent on getting Joseph to yield but praise the Lord he did not. Where are his likes today? Are you one of them?

She seemed to have changed her tactics and said to him,

> "If you will not lie with me, just stay with me. Just play with me but do not go the whole way".

This was a slow way of accomplishing her aim and Joseph was wise enough to reject it. He saw ahead of time what was in view. He knew that if he gave in to being with her, he might reach a point when he would be off guard and fall. So he refused completely. Here was perfect wisdom for no sin is committed at once. It is the small beginnings, looking so innocent, that are most dangerous. It may just be a look, a handshake, a careless word, a careless touch and these can finally lead to the destruction of a brilliant career. The best thing to do with sin is to overcome it at the very beginning. My dear friend, are you playing with some sin? From the beginning it appears apparently innocent, but do you hear the small warnings from conscience that tell you that the Lord is not a part of it? Would you hearken at once? Friend, I beg you in the name of Jesus to stop. The price of folly is too great for you to have to pay it. Others may have done the same thing and not received permanent damage. Can you afford even the slightest damage that this may cause in your relationship with the Lord? Joseph was wise. He would not listen to her, to lie with her or to be with her! Glory be to the Lord! May the Lord raise many such young men and women in the Body of Christ. They are urgently needed. Lord, in your might and power, raise them.

There are a number of human reasons why Joseph ought to have yielded to Potiphar's wife. First of all, she was the mistress of the house. He could have said, "I am just a slave-servant. My duty demands that I obey her." Of course, he did not follow that kind of reasoning because he was bound by a higher demand of obedience—the demand of the Lord. He obeyed the higher law—the higher authority. May we too do the same when faced with conflicting demands.

Secondly, no one would ever discover what he had done. She was the mistress of the house. She would arrange the circumstances well so that discovery would be impossible. Joseph however, knew that there could be a hiding from man but never a hiding from God. God sees even in the darkest night. He sees behind closed doors. He will judge the secrets of men. Everything done in the dark will be revealed. Joseph feared God.

Thirdly, this sin could have led to his promotion. He was already Potiphar's favourite servant. If he yielded and became Mrs Potiphar's favourite "lover", his position in the house would probably have been set forever. Yes, his position would have been established but what position? The position as a slave-servant! His vision would have been brought to naught by his sin. Joseph rejected the sin.

Fourthly, the sin came in day by day. He could have said, "I have tried my best. From now on, if anything happens, it is entirely her fault". He must have thought in the pattern of the following scriptures,

> *No temptation has overtaken you that is not common to man. God is faithful, and he will not let you be tempted beyond your strength, but with the temptation will also provide the way of escape, that you may be able to endure it* (1 Corinthians 10:13).

Yes, there is a way out. Your boss may be tempting you. It may look as if your promotion depends on your yielding but, fellow saint, don't yield. There is a way of escape. God can promote you against the wishes of your boss, but if not, yielding to the temptation means that you remain unpromoted. It is better to occupy the lowest position in your job with a clear conscience than to be a hell-going boss.

In a final desperate attempt, she seized him and wanted to force him to sin. He ran away and bore the consequence.

Let me say very clearly that in this matter of sexual purity, there are very few who are upholding the standard of the Lord. Many are not involved in acts but they harbour and enjoy impure thoughts. That is most serious before God who demands purity in the inward parts. Saint of God, let me ask you a very personal question, "Are your thoughts pure?" If your thoughts are not pure your heart is impure and the Lord said,

> *Blessed are the pure in heart, for they shall see God* (Matthew 5:8).

Strive for peace with all men, and for the holiness without which no one will see the Lord (Hebrews 12:14).

The Holy Spirit must be allowed to work out this purification, sanctification and deliverance from the very centre of the being. Only such pure vessels can satisfy His heart in service. The Lord's work suffers very much because the average believer is far from pure.

Your thoughts can be rendered pure. Jesus saves to the uttermost. His is a full and free salvation. Do you want it? Will you let go so that He may carry out a fresh work in you? The apostle says,

If any one purifies himself from that which is ignoble (and all sin is ignoble) *then he will be a vessel for noble use, consecrated and useful to the maker of the house, ready for any good work."* (2 Timothy 2:21).

3. SUFFERING WITHOUT COMPLAINT

Joseph overcame temptation in God's rating, but before man he was an absolute failure. This is why the temptation was so fierce. He knew that no one would ever believe his version of the story. He still did not yield even though he knew he would be painted so badly. He was content to be justified before God. He did not care what popular opinion was. He only knew that he had to be faithful to his Lord and that one day, he would receive the heavenly Master's commendation, "Well done, good and faithful servant".

Oh, may God deliver you from wooing the commendations of men. May God deliver me from wooing the commendations of men. May we all, as servants of the Lord of glory, be prepared to leave everything in God's hands and wait for that day of reckoning. May we leave not only our own work and conduct with Him, but also the work and conduct of others. The apostle Paul says,

> *But with me it is a very small thing that I should be judged by you or by any human court. I do not even judge myself. I am not aware of anything against myself, but I am not thereby acquitted. It is the Lord who judges me. Therefore do not pronounce judgment before the time, before the Lord comes, who will bring to light the things now hidden in darkness and will disclose the purposes of the heart. Then every man will receive his commendation from God* (1 Corinthians 4:3–5)

Potiphar's wife, whose conscience was dead spoke out but Joseph did not speak. He could have spoken out even if no one would believe him, yet he did not speak. He did not want to expose his master's wife, guilty as she was. He preferred to suffer as a criminal. Joseph had really made progress in the way of the cross which is also the way of the Lord Jesus. He covered up the sins of others and bore the penalty for it. I just feel condemned by the greatness of Joseph's heart. He was truly fit to rule. May the Lord have mercy on me and may the cross carry out a deeper work in my own life. Joseph was truly like the Lord whom the Bible says,

> *He was oppressed, and he was afflicted, yet he opened not his mouth; like a lamb that is led to the slaughter, and like a sheep that before its shearers is dumb, so he opened not his mouth* (Isaiah 53:7).

The great need of the church is that God would raise such men and women. I am not yet one such, but Oh, that God would transform me into one such. That is my cry.

4. THE UNFORSAKEN PRISONER

Prison is a lonely place. It is even more lonely for the one who suffers innocently. It was not easy for Joseph. His was one unending path of suffering for righteousness yet he did not complain. It must have caused him more pain to read what was written on his prison card as his crime, "an unsuccessful adulterer".

How unlike his character was this label! Yet he bore it. Some can bear shame for a short time but only the Lord's choicest servants can bear prolonged suffering and shame without complaining. Joseph was one such.

God is God. His companionship is great. The Psalmist could say,

> *Even though I walk through the valley of the shadow of death, I fear no evil; for thou art with me; thy rod and thy staff, they comfort me* (Psalm 23:4).

Yes, "thou art with me" and it makes all the difference. Suffering saint, the Lord is with thee. You are not alone. May His presence brighten your prison cell, your dark circumstances. So the Bible says,

> *But the LORD was with Joseph and showed him steadfast love, and gave him favor in the sight of the keeper of the prison* (Genesis 39:21).

Joseph was in prison but he was truly rich. He was rich with imperishable riches, the Lord's presence, the Lord's steadfast love, God-created favour in the sight of the keeper of the prison. These are enough. Someday, you the reader and I the writer may be jailed because of our testimony for the Lord

Jesus. When that time comes, may we not seek earthly comfort and passing treasure. May the Lord grant us His constant presence, steadfast love and favour with prison authorities so that even there we may bring others into the kingdom.

The favour that God granted Joseph before the prison guard bore fruit. The Bible says,

> *And the keeper of the prison committed to Joseph's care all the prisoners who were in the prison; and whatever was done there, he was the doer of it; the keeper of the prison paid no heed to anything that was in Joseph's care because the LORD was with him; and whatever he did, the LORD made it prosper* (Genesis 39:22,23).

So even in prison, because of the Lord's help, Joseph was in leadership. The Lord was gradually, step by step, training him for his future responsibilities. God will not put untried and untrained people into places of responsibility. When the need arises, He will send them to prison and use the prison as a training school for leadership in His divine programmes. The Lord Jesus is coming back soon to establish His glorious kingdom. He will place people in rulership who have been through His training schools. The most important leadership school is "The school of suffering;" and the principal is Madam Suffering. Jesus was once a student in that school and He graduated with flying colours, stamping His personality on everything in that school. He is now in rulership. All prospective rulers with Him must enrol in that school and leave their marks there too. Have you enrolled in that school? How long have you been there? (The best students are allowed to stay there longer, in order to take advanced courses on suffering. Such courses are indispensable for high level rulership in the coming kingdom). Are you destroying your grades by complaining while suffering? (Distinctions are won for severe suffering borne with much rejoicing). The Lord of glory says,

*Blessed are you when men revile you and persecute you and utter all kinds of evil against you falsely on my account. **Rejoice and be glad**, for your reward is great in heaven, for so men persecuted the prophets who were before you* (Matthew 5:11, 12).

THE FORGOTTEN PRISONER

Some time after this, the butler of the king of Egypt and his baker offended their lord the king of Egypt. And Pharaoh was angry with his two officers, the chief butler and the chief baker, and he put them in custody in the house of the captain of the guard, in the prison where Joseph was confined. The captain of the guard charged Joseph with them, and he waited on them; and they continued for some time in custody. And one night they both dreamed--the butler and the baker of the king of Egypt, who were confined in the prison-- each his own dream, and each dream with its own meaning. When Joseph came to them in the morning and saw them, they were troubled. So he asked Pharaoh's officers who were with him in custody in his master's house, "Why are your faces downcast today?" They said to him, "We have had dreams, and there is no one to interpret them." And Joseph said to them, "Do not interpretations belong to God? Tell them to me, I pray you."

So the chief butler told his dream to Joseph, and said to him, "In my dream there was a vine before me, and on the vine there were three branches; as soon as it budded, its blossoms shot forth, and the clusters ripened into grapes. Pharaoh's cup was in my hand; and I took the grapes and pressed them into Pharaoh's cup, and placed the cup in Pharaoh's hand." Then Joseph said to him, "This is its interpretation: the three branches are three days; within three days Pharaoh will lift up your head and restore you to your office; and you shall place Pharaoh's cup in his hand as formerly, when you were his butler. But remember me, when it is well with you, and do me the kindness, I pray you, to make mention of me to Pharaoh, and so get me out of this house. For I was indeed stolen out of the land of the Hebrews; and here also I have done nothing that they should put me into the dungeon."

When the chief baker saw that the interpretation was favorable, he said to Joseph, "I also had a dream: there were three cake baskets on my head, and in the uppermost basket there were all sorts of baked food for Pharaoh, but the birds were eating it out of the basket on my head." And Joseph answered, "This is its interpretation: the three baskets are three days; within three days Pharaoh will lift up your head--from you!--and hang you on a tree; and the birds will eat the flesh from you."

On the third day, which was Pharaoh's birthday, he made a feast for all his servants, and lifted up the head of the chief butler and the head of the chief baker among his servants. He restored the chief butler to his butlership, and he placed the cup in Pharaoh's hand; but he hanged the chief baker, as Joseph had interpreted to them. Yet the chief butler did not remember Joseph, but forgot him (Genesis 40:1–23).

Joseph made progress in prison. He interpreted the dreams of Pharaoh's butler and baker. The interpretations came true. The baker was hanged on a tree and the butler restored to his position. It is here that Joseph committed the two visible errors of his life.

The first error is that he solicited human help. All through his life, in trials and suffering he never appealed to man for help. He did not appeal to his brothers to spare his life or not to sell him. He did not appeal to Potiphar to reason with him and set him free because he was innocent. He had depended on God all his life and God had not failed him.

Now in prison he begins to appeal to man. He said to the butler, *But remember me, when it is well with you, and do me kindness, I pray you, to make mention of me to Pharaoh, and so get me out of this house* (Genesis 40:14). He appealed to man. He wanted man to remember him. He wanted man to do him kindness. He wanted man to mention him to Pharaoh. He wanted to be taken out of the school of suffering prematurely. This was a serious character defect. He made it appear as if the Lord who was with him could not get him out of the place. He even called the place not a prison but a dungeon. This must certainly have been a point of grave weakness. He turned from God to man, he took to human methods to replace divine ones. He sort of went to Egypt for help as the Bible says,

"Woe to the rebellious children," says the LORD, "who carry out a plan, but not mine; and who make a league, but not of my spirit, that they may add sin to sin; who set out to go down to Egypt, without asking for my counsel, to take refuge in the protection of Pharaoh, and to seek shelter in the shadow of Egypt! (Isaiah 30:1,2).

This was Joseph's first fault.

His second fault was that he complained,

For I was indeed stolen out of the land of the Hebrews; and here also I have done nothing that should put me into the dungeon (Genesis 40:15).

God knew his story well. God was taking care of him. Why did he need to complain to man? This was bad. May we learn through much suffering to be different. May we be completely delivered from complaining and from pleading our cause with man. God alone is sufficient. May we learn to confide in Him and only in Him. He knows. At the right time, after we have learnt all the necessary lessons, He will act on our behalf.

Although Joseph solicited the butler's help, this solicitation was in vain. The butler was released,

> *Yet the chief butler did not remember Joseph, but forgot him* (Genesis 40:23).

How futile human help is! How undependable is man's help!! The butler forgot him. What happened to Joseph's request? It went to the winds. God had set Joseph aside to be peculiarly and exclusively His own and He would not allow Joseph to receive any blessings that He did not Himself design for him. God is jealous about all the special vessels in His training school and He will not let them have their way even for a moment.

The present behaviour of Joseph showed God that although he had already spent much time in the school of suffering, his training there was not yet complete and he must not be allowed to graduate then. So the Lord ensured that Joseph spent another two whole years in prison:

> *After two whole years, Pharaoh dreamed ...* (Genesis 41:1).

Was God being very hard? No, never! God is most tender but God also wants perfect vessels that will fulfil His highest purpose. There are no short-cuts with God.

Have you been suffering for long? Maybe you are a very choice vessel and that is why the Lord has prolonged your stay in the school of suffering. He is watching over your programme carefully and planning your courses all by Himself. He will not allow one second more of suffering than you actually need to reach His perfection. When that place of perfection is reached, He will bring you out at once and throughout the years of your rulership, you will see more clearly why every second of your long stay there was necessary. Glory be to Him.

FROM PRISON TO THE THRONE

Then the chief butler said to Pharaoh, "I remember my faults today. When Pharaoh was angry with his servants, and put me and the chief baker in custody in the house of the captain of the guard, we dreamed on the same night, he and I, each having a dream with its own meaning. A young Hebrew was there with us, a servant of the captain of the guard; and when we told him, he interpreted our dreams to us, giving an interpretation to each man according to his dream. And as he interpreted to us, so it came to pass; I was restored to my office, and the baker was hanged."

Then Pharaoh sent and called Joseph, and they brought him hastily out of the dungeon; and when he had shaved himself and changed his clothes, he came in before Pharaoh. And Pharaoh said to Joseph, "I have had a dream, and there is no one who can interpret it; and I have heard it said of you that when you hear a dream you can interpret it." Joseph answered Pharaoh, "It is not in me; God will give Pharaoh a favorable answer" (Genesis 41:9–16).

1. GOD'S PERFECT TIMING

The butler forgot Joseph for two years but God was in control of it all, for His time had not yet come. This matter of God's time is of the utmost importance in our relationship and our service for Him. The Lord Jesus told his brothers,

> *...My hour has not yet come...* (John 2:4).

The apostle Paul said,

> *But when the time had fully come, God sent forth His Son...* (Galatians 4:4).

We see clearly that God has a perfect time for each of His deeds and actions. He does not only have deeds and actions; He has apportioned to each a perfect time. The right action, done at the wrong time will produce disastrous results! All who serve the Lord must not only receive from the Lord what they are to do but they must equally and clearly receive from the Lord when they are to do it. Much harm is caused by carnal haste or carnal delay. Many have rushed on into some service which the Lord intended for them well ahead of His time for that project and failed woefully, not because God did not originate the project, but because God's time for it had not yet come. Others have waited and delayed until God's time was past and they went ahead only to meet disastrous failure.

To be in the centre of God's will means that you know at least the following four things:

1. what He wants done
2. when He wants it done
3. where He wants it done and
4. how He wants it done.

If we settle these things clearly before Him, we shall save ourselves a lot of unnecessary heartache and cause less confusion to God's work.

Joseph had tried earlier to be released. If his desire then had materialised and the butler had helped him to be released, he would have been freed from prison but he would have been nothing more than a freed slave. God's timing was associated with God's plans to waft him to greatness and glory. My beloved saint, do not be in a hurry to rush ahead and destroy the wonderful plan that God has for your greatness. Is your problem marriage? Please, do not just rush ahead and marry anyone just because you are lonely. Later on, you will meet God's perfect choice for you and what would you do when you are already wrongly yoked even to the wrong Christian partner? I beg you to wait. God will always act on time. Is God calling you to some service now which you want to postpone because of some earthly pleasure—marriage, education, fame, money? Please act at once. The opportunity which God has for you today may never repeat itself. Won't you obey?

When God's time was fully come, the chief butler remembered Joseph (Genesis 41:9-13). God had at last acted and He had acted on time and Joseph would soon access a position of honour and glory. Praise the Lord.

2. JOSEPH INTERPRETS PHARAOH'S DREAMS

Joseph is now before Pharaoh. He had shaved and changed clothes. Imprisonment was now in the past but what did the future hold? That lay in God's hands and the Almighty would surely handle it well. He who had been with Joseph throughout would surely stand by him now to settle the matter of his future. Pharaoh talked to Joseph about his ability to interpret dreams. The emphasis was on Joseph's ability. Joseph, knowing where the source of his wisdom came from, would not take God's glory for himself. He immediately said to Pharaoh, It is not in me; God will give Pharaoh a favourable answer (Genesis 41:16). "It is not in me; God will give..." These are the marks of true humility. Joseph had truly made progress. Not in me but God! That is greatness!

Joseph then interpreted the dreams and then offered Pharaoh God-given counsel. The slave-prisoner was now the adviser of the king of Egypt. How wonderful! This was all the Lord's doing and greatly is He to be praised. God is able to do the impossible. Let us trust Him without doubting. Let us submit our ways to Him and follow His leading and in due time He will exalt us, if not in this world, then in His kingdom.

3. JOSEPH ON THE THRONE

Pharaoh was not only content to have Joseph as his counsellor. He exalted Joseph to the place of greatest power in Egypt next only to himself. It was popular consent. The Bible says,

> *This proposal seemed good to Pharaoh and to all his servants* (Genesis 41:37).

When God brings someone to rulership, He arranges events to ensure that the person is accepted. A wonderful scene now follows. Do not miss it. The Bible says,

So Pharaoh said to Joseph, "Since God has shown you all these, there is none so discreet and wise as you are; you shall be over my house, and all my people shall order themselves as you command; only as regards the throne will I be greater than you." And Pharaoh said to Joseph, "Behold, I have set you over all the land of Egypt." Then Pharaoh took his signet ring from his hand and put it on Joseph's hand and arrayed him in garments of fine linen, and put a gold chain about his neck; and he made him ride in his second chariot; and they cried before him, "Bow the knee!" Thus he set him over all the land of Egypt (Genesis 41:39–43).

Joseph was now glorified. His training in suffering was over. Joseph was thirty years old, then thirteen years since he first saw the vision of his greatness. It had taken time but it had come to pass at last. God is faithful. His word will never go unfulfilled. Another seven years were to elapse before his brothers would bow to him but that too was surely going to be fulfilled.

God is not a man, that he should lie, or a son of man, that he should repent. Has he said, and will he not do it? Or has he spoken, and will he not fulfil it? (Numbers 23:19).

● 4

THE GREATNESS OF JOSEPH

1. JOSEPH AND HIS BROTHERS: THE IMPERISHABILITY OF SIN

Joseph's brothers had sinned against him. For twenty years they had never repented of their sin. Time had passed but their sin remained. Time will never take away sin. We shall be faced with all our unconfessed sins at the judgement seat of Christ and give account for them.

Joseph's brothers journeyed to Egypt to buy grain. They came face to face with none other than their brother Joseph whom they had sold away twenty years before. They came and bowed themselves before him with their faces to the ground (Genesis 42:6). The prophecy had come true.

They now could not forget their sin.

Then they said to one another, "In truth we are guilty concerning our brother, in that we saw the distress of his soul, when he besought us and we would not listen; therefore is this distress come upon us".

And Reuben answered them, "Did I not tell you not to sin against the lad? But you would not listen. So now there comes a reckoning for his blood" (Genesis 42:21,22).

Yes, there comes a reckoning! A reckoning will come for each unconfessed sin on that day. As you live your life, take that into daily account for as the apostle Paul puts it,

On that day when, according to my gospel, God judges the secrets of men by Christ Jesus (Romans 2:16).

Joseph was putting them on temporary trial but how painful it was for him. He had grown very deep in the knowledge of the Lord and his heart had grown tender, very tender. He wept (Genesis 42:23). May God enable us to grow in tenderness as we grow in grace. May He take away any youthful and carnal harshness.

2. JOSEPH AND HIS BROTHERS: JOSEPH FORGIVES GRACIOUSLY

Finally, Joseph discloses himself to his brothers. It was an emotion-packed event.

"... I am Joseph; is my father still alive"... (Genesis 45:3).

... "Come near to me I pray you."... (Genesis 45:4).

..."I am your brother, Joseph, whom you sold to Egypt. And now do not be distressed or angry with yourselves, because you sold me here; for God sent me before you to preserve life" (Genesis 45:4–5).

Only a truly great man could say to those who tried to kill him and finally sold him into slavery and suffering, "Do not be distressed or angry with yourselves for what you did to me."

Only a very great heart could forgive so completely and instead comfort those who did great wrong. May God grant each one of us such greatness.

3. JOSEPH AND HIS BROTHERS: THE SOVEREIGN GOD

Joseph did not only forgive and comfort his brothers. He saw beyond their wickedness the mighty sovereign God. He said the following far-reaching words,

> *God sent me before you to preserve for you a remnant on earth, and to keep alive for you many survivors. So it was not you who sent me here, but God; and He has made me a father to Pharaoh, and lord of all his house and ruler over all the land of Egypt* (Genesis 45:7,8).

Later on, when their father was dead and they feared that he might revenge, he said the same thing to them,

> *...Fear not, for am I in the place of God? As for you, you meant evil against me; but God meant it for good, to bring it about that many people should be kept alive, as they are today* (Genesis 50:19,20).

Joseph saw the hand of God. True enough his brothers had evil intentions but God was working out His own purpose. Their purpose was wicked—to please self. God's purpose was great—to preserve much life. So Joseph saw himself merely as God's servant in Egypt. He was merely servant in God's purpose. God sent me before you; God sent me to preserve for you a remnant on earth; God sent me to keep alive for you many survivors. Do you notice the frequency of you, you, you? The ones who deserved the greatest punishment instead received great blessing.

"It was not you who sent me here, but God." This is true knowledge. Mature saints through the generations sometimes reached the same pinnacle of growth and surrendered to the overruling purposes of God. They willingly refused to deal with secondary causes. They refused to blame either man or their circumstances and such have entered into the rest of God. There is nothing as disturbing as to be dissatisfied with one's circumstances. There is nothing that hurts the Lord as a grumbling, questioning and restless heart. May we all know through yielding that

> *...In everything God works for good with those who love him, who are called according his purpose* (Romans 8:28).

We just need to be sure that we love Him and whatever our circumstances may be, even if they apparently are horrible, we know that God will work them out for our ultimate good. May we like Joseph, have unshakeable confidence in the Lord's goodness even while all around is dark. May we say with Job,

> *...The LORD gave, and the LORD has taken away, blessed be the name of the LORD* (Job 1:21).

5

─────────────

THE SECRET OF JOSEPH'S GREATNESS

─────────────

*J*oseph certainly went far with God. He went further than most saints have gone. He went far in submission to the sovereignty of God and his character was close to irreproachable. We cannot help but ask, "What was his secret?" What must we do if we too, like him, are to become men after God's own heart?

1. FIRST SECRET: THE LORD WAS WITH HIM

I believe that the secret to his life's success lay in a sentence that comes up frequently in the biblical account of his life. It is this:

"The LORD was with Joseph and..." (Genesis 39:2)

"But the LORD was with Joseph and..." (Genesis 39:21)

"The LORD was with him and..." (Genesis 39:23)

The Lord was with Joseph in all his circumstances, however dark they were. Joseph walked close to the Lord. He sought God's will. He surrendered his will absolutely to God's will and so the Lord made him a special companion. The Lord therefore guided him and blessed all his endeavours.

2. SECOND SECRET: JOSEPH RECOGNIZED HIS POSITION AS LEADER NO. 2

The Leader No. 1 is the man of the vision; he sees the vision; he receives the vision from God and says:

> "We must get to such a place on such a date. These are the resources needed to get there"

and the leader No. 2 makes all the arrangements, searching for the right people, putting the structures together, sleeping neither during the day nor during the night in order to lead people to the place indicated by the leader No. 1. Unfortunately, many leader No. 2s do not know what it is all about.

Pharaoh was the leader No. 1. God had shown him the vision of what was to happen in Egypt. He had received the revelation that there would be seven years of abundance and seven years of famine. Joseph was the leader No. 2 who acted upon the vision to ensure that the nation did not perish. When people needed food, they didn't go to Pharaoh but rather to Joseph. Joseph was the manager. Even in a store, there is a proprietor and there is a manager, isn't there? The owner can sleep. The manager does not work for himself, but for the owner. If the leader N° 2 does not work for the leader No. 1, he is a Judas.

3. THIRD SECRET: JOSEPH THE LOYAL NO. 2

The leader No. 2 is loyal or else he has cursed himself and God will remove him.

> *Joseph collected all the money that was to be found in Egypt and Canaan in payment for the grain they were buying, and he brought it to Pharaoh's palace* (Genesis 47:14, NIV).

"So Joseph bought all the land in Egypt for Pharaoh. The Egyptians, one and all, sold their fields, because the famine was too severe for them. The land became Pharaohs" (Genesis 47: 20, NIV)

Joseph acquired nothing for himself. All the land became Pharaoh's property. All the money became Pharaoh's money.

Joseph said to the people,

> *"Now that I have bought you and your land today for Pharaoh, here is seed for you so you can plant the ground"* (Genesis 47:23, NIV).

Money, land and the people became Pharaoh's property. This is the work of the leader No. 2.

Who is your Pharaoh?

Let me ask you a question:

"Who is your Pharaoh?"

You cannot serve in the capacity of Pharaoh when you have not been serving in the capacity of Joseph.

Who is your Pharaoh? I am asking you the question now so that you may give an answer to God; so that you may give yourself an answer, so that you may give an answer to those of us who are here.

Who is your Pharaoh? If you don't have a Pharaoh, you are a rebel and God will ensure that you don't have a Joseph and if they are raised, God will scatter them.

Who is your Pharaoh? If you are independent, you are in the centre of sin. Who is your Pharaoh? To whom has God given the vision?

Joseph was very spiritual; but God did not give him the vision. If Joseph's heart were wrong, he would have had every reason to convince the people not to submit to Pharaoh, but Joseph's heart was right. Did God make a mistake by giving the vision to Pharaoh?

4. FOURTH SECRET: GOD'S SOVEREIGN CHOICE

> *Invite Jesse to the sacrifice, and I will show you what to do. You are to anoint for me the one I indicate* (1 Samuel 16:3, NIV).

The supreme leader is anointed by God, when you begin to question God saying:

> "Why do you choose this one?"

You are preparing your destruction because you have dared to raise your hand against the Throne. There is confusion in churches, assemblies, because people do not ask themselves:

> "Who has God chosen? Who is the Pharaoh here?"

Blessed are you, if you understand this, but if you don't understand this, may God have mercy on you. If you don't understand, you are operating with the spirit of Miriam (Moses' sister) who said:

"Has the Lord spoken only through Moses?"

And as reward for her questioning, she had leprosy. She thought that spiritual leadership was a family issue. It is God who chooses the Pharaoh. When God chooses you to be Joseph and you instead covet Pharaoh's role forgetting that this work is not given by man, all your life will be confused.

That was the apex of Joseph's life. This is where the greatness of his heart was manifested. The vision! The vision!! The vision!!!

There is only one question to ask: "To whom has the vision been given?"

Joseph could interpret dreams, but God refused to give him the vision. God chose Pharaoh and gave him the vision and by so doing placed Joseph under Pharaoh's authority and made Joseph his servant. So, Joseph brought all the lands of Egypt and all the people to Pharaoh.

This day, I have used words I have never used in my life. I know about Joseph serving Pharaoh. But, this is the first time; I am talking about the question, "Who has the vision?"

And the matter of the vision being the possession of the supreme manager, my knowledge about it in the past was very shallow.

AN EXAMPLE OF PASTOR ENOCH ADEBOYE

I want to talk a little bit about something that does not exist in our ministry. There is a minister of God in Nigeria called

Pastor Enoch Adeboye. He is the leading pastor of the Redeemed Christian Church of God. He produces daily devotionals (i.e. a book that has a meditation in the Scripture for each day of the year). I read a production that enabled me to know the man for who he is. He is a very grounded man of God, a consecrated man. He may have problems; they may be doing funny things. (I insist that, they may be doing funny things) but the man I met in my readings day after day for 365 days is a consecrated man. He knows God and he walks with Him. He is the most striking example of a Joseph that exists in our days. The founder of this ministry (the Redeemed Christian Church of God) was an illiterate and the pastor I am talking about is a PhD holder in Mathematics. Pastor Adeboye followed the vision of this man whom he calls "Baba" (Daddy), without compromising. Even long after he had died, Pastor Adeboye is following the vision of "Baba" (Daddy). This is what I am saying. Even after "Baba" (Daddy) had died, Pastor Adeboye is following the vision. And he has been unusually blessed.

He has not tried to be another Pharaoh; he has not sought for another vision, he has not created his personal vision.

There cannot be two visions.

Dr. Adeboye knows that there is only one vision for the people he leads, that God had given this vision to that old man, and that his own duty is to spread it in the whole world and he is succeeding.

AFTERWORD

Joseph gave God the first place. In everything, he joyfully accepted his position of leader No. 2. His success stems first of all, from the unfailing presence of God with him, a presence that was made possible by his faithful commitment to obedience and to truth.

His success also originates from God's sovereign choice. We must all understand that for any work, there is only one Pharaoh whom we must look up to, but that, there can be a Joseph No. 1, a Joseph No. 2, a Joseph No. 3, and so on. If we don't understand this there will be great confusion in the work because every missionary will settle in the nation to which he is sent as a Pharaoh. Yet if a missionary establishes himself as Pharaoh, there will be consequences; he may block the money claiming that he is already Pharaoh. He may also block men saying that they have already come to Pharaoh. He will then make himself Pharaoh of the nation.

Our prayer is that every leader receive the revelation about who is Pharaoh and who is Joseph and that he would joyfully accept God's sovereign choice.

BACK MATTERS

VERY IMPORTANT!!!

If you have not yet received Jesus as your Lord and Saviour, I encourage you to receive Him. Here are some steps to help you,

ADMIT that you are a sinner by nature and by practice and that on your own you are without hope. Tell God you have personally sinned against Him in your thoughts, words and deeds. Confess your sins to Him, one after another in a sincere prayer. Do not leave out any sins that you can remember. Truly turn from your sinful ways and abandon them. If you stole, steal no more. If you have been committing adultery or fornication, stop it. God will not forgive you if you have no desire to stop sinning in all areas of your life, but if you are sincere, He will give you the power to stop sinning.

BELIEVE that Jesus Christ, who is God's Son, is the only Way, the only Truth and the only Life. Jesus said,

"I am the way, the truth and the life; no one comes to the Father, but by me" (John 14:6).

The Bible says,

> *"For there is one God, and there is one mediator between God and men, the man Christ Jesus, who gave himself as a ransom for all"* (1 Timothy 2:5-6).

> *"And there is salvation in no one else (apart from Jesus), for there is no other name under heaven given among men by which we must be saved"* (Acts 4:12).

> *But to all who received him, who believed in his name, he gave power to become children of God..."* (John 1:12).

BUT,

CONSIDER the cost of following Him. Jesus said that all who follow Him must deny themselves, and this includes selfish financial, social and other interests. He also wants His followers to take up their crosses and follow Him. Are you prepared to abandon your own interests daily for those of Christ? Are you prepared to be led in a new direction by Him? Are you prepared to suffer for Him and die for Him if need be? Jesus will have nothing to do with half-hearted people. His demands are total. He will only receive and forgive those who are prepared to follow Him AT ANY COST. Think about it and count the cost. If you are prepared to follow Him, come what may, then there is something to do.

INVITE Jesus to come into your heart and life. He says,

> *"Behold I stand at the door and knock. If anyone hears my voice and opens the door (to his heart and life), I will come in to him and eat with him, and he with me "* (Revelation 3:20).

Why don't you pray a prayer like the following one or one of your own construction as the Holy Spirit leads?

> "Lord Jesus, I am a wretched, lost sinner who
> has sinned in thought, word and deed.
> Forgive all my sins and cleanse me. Receive
> me, Saviour and transform me into a child
> of God. Come into my heart now and give
> me eternal life right now. I will follow you at
> all costs, trusting the Holy Spirit to give me
> all the power I need."

When you pray this prayer sincerely, Jesus answers at once and justifies you before God and makes you His child.

*Please write to us (**ztfbooks@cmfionline.org**) and I will pray for you and help you as you go on with Jesus Christ.*

THANK YOU

For Reading This Book

If you have any question and/or need help, do not hesitate to contact us through **ztfbooks@cmfionline.org**. If the book has blessed you, then we would also be grateful if you leave a positive review at your favorite retailer.

ZTF BOOKS, through the Book Ministry of Christian Missionary Fellowship International (CMFI) offers a wide selection of best selling Christian books (in print, eBook & audiobook formats) on a broad spectrum of topics, including marriage & family, sexuality, practical spiritual warfare, Christian service, Christian leadership, and much more. Visit us at **ztfbooks.com** to learn more about our latest releases and special offers. And thank you for being a ZTF BOOK reader.

We invite you to connect with more from the author through social media (**cmfionline**) and/or ministry website (**ztfministry.org**), where we offer both on-ground and remote training courses (all year round) from basic to university level at the University of Prayer and Fasting (WUPF) and the School of Knowing and Serving God (SKSG). You are highly welcome to enrol at your soonest convenience. A FREE online Bible Course is also available.

We would like to recommend to you the next book in this series: Spiritual Leadership in the Pattern of David

David was anything but perfect—lustful as a husband, weak as a father, and partial as a leader—

yet he is the only one in all Scripture to be called *"a man after God's own heart"*.

What was it in David that attracted God this much?

After the historic victory with Goliath, the life of this humble shepherd boy seemingly took a downward turn. In all the series of unfortunate circumstances, God was at work, rerouting his life. Starting with a group of riff-raff, this cave dweller became the leader of an exceptional army because God wanted him to become <u>a maverick king</u>:

- In battle, he modeled invincibility.
- In decisions, he sought God's mind for clarity, wisdom, and equity.
- In loneliness, he wrote with transparent vulnerability and quiet trust.
- In friendship, he was loyal to the end.
- In statesmanship, he portrayed integrity and humility.

What an outstanding man! **But what is it that distinguished David as one of God's greatest men?**

Come along with professor *Z.T. Fomum* in this down-to-earth book on *Spiritual Leadership*, for <u>an in-depth study on the making of this poet, musician, courageous warrior, and shepherd of God's people</u>—a man of passion and destiny with a God-dependent life of strength and leadership worth emulating.

ABOUT THE AUTHOR

Professor Zacharias Tanee Fomum was born in the flesh on 20th June 1945 and became born again on 13th June 1956. On 1st October 1966, He consecrated his life to the Lord Jesus and to His service, and was filled with the Holy Spirit on 24th October 1970. He was taken to be with the Lord on 14th March, 2009.

Pr Fomum was admitted to a first class in the Bachelor of Science degree, graduating as a prize winning student from Fourah Bay College in the University of Sierra Leone in October 1969. At the age of 28, he was awarded a Ph.D. in Organic Chemistry by the University of Makerere, Kampala in Uganda. In October 2005, he was awarded a Doctor of Science (D.Sc) by the University of Durham, Great Britain. This higher doctorate was in recognition of his distinct contributions to scientific knowledge through research. As a Professor of Organic Chemistry in the University of Yaoundé 1, Cameroon, Professor Fomum supervised or co-supervised more than 100 Master's Degree and Doctoral Degree theses and co-authored over 160 scientific articles in leading international journals. He considered Jesus Christ the Lord of Science ("For by Him all things were created..." – Colossians 1:16), and scientific research an act of obedience to God's command to "subdue the earth" (Genesis 1:28). He therefore made the Lord Jesus the Director of his research laboratory while he took the place of deputy director, and attributed his outstanding success as a scientist to Jesus' revelational leadership.

In more than 40 years of Christian ministry, Pr Fomum travelled extensively, preaching the Gospel, planting churches and training spiritual leaders. He made more than:

- 700 missionary journeys within Cameroon, which ranged from one day to three weeks in duration.
- 500 missionary journeys to more than 70 different nations in all the six continents. These ranged from two days to six weeks in duration.

By the time of his going to be with the Lord in 2009, he had preached in over 1000 localities in Cameroon, sent over 200 national missionaries into many localities in Cameroon and planted over 1300 churches in the various administrative provinces of Cameroon. At his base in Yaoundé, he planted and built a mega-church with his co-workers which grew to a steady membership of about 12,000. Pr Fomum was the founding team-leader of Christian Missionary Fellowship International (CMFI); an evangelism, soul-winning, disciple making, Church-planting and missionary-sending movement with more than 200 international missionaries and thousands of churches in 65 nations spread across Africa, Europe, the Americas, Asia and Oceania. In the course of their ministry, Pr Fomum and his team witnessed more than 10,000 recorded healing miracles performed by God in answer to prayer in the name of Jesus Christ. These miracles include instant healings of headaches, cancers, HIV/AIDS, blindness, deafness, dumbness, paralysis, madness, and new teeth and organs received.

Pr Fomum read the entire Bible more than 60 times, read more than 1350 books on the Christian faith and authored over 150 books to advance the Gospel of Jesus Christ. 5 million copies of these books are in circulation in 12 languages as well as 16 million gospel tracts in 17 languages.

Pr Fomum was a man who sought God. He spent between 15 minutes and six hours daily alone with God in what he called Daily Dynamic Encounters with God (DDEWG). During these DDEWG he read God's Word, meditated on it, listened to God's voice, heard God speak to him, recorded what God was saying to him and prayed it through. He thus had over 18,000 DDEWG. He also had over 60 periods of withdrawing to seek God alone for periods that ranged from 3 to 21 days (which he termed Retreats for Spiritual Progress). The time he spent seeking God slowly transformed him into a man who hungered, thirsted and panted after God. His unceasing heart cry was: "Oh, that I would have more of God!"

Pr Fomum was a man of prayer and a leading teacher on prayer in many churches and conferences around the world. He considered prayer to be the most important work that can be done for God and for man. He was a man of faith who believed that God answers prayer. He kept a record of his prayer requests and had over 50, 000 recorded answers to prayer in his prayer books. He carried out over 100 Prayer Walks of between five and forty-seven kilometres in towns and cities around the world. He and his team carried out over 57 Prayer Crusades (periods of forty days and nights during which at least eight hours are invested into prayer each day). They also carried out over 80 Prayer Sieges (times of near non-stop praying that ranges from 24 hours to 120 hours). He authored the Prayer Power Series, a 13-volume set of books on various aspects of prayer; Supplication, Fasting, Intercession and Spiritual Warfare. He started prayer chains, prayer rooms, prayer houses, national and continental prayer movements in Cameroon and other nations. He worked with leaders of local churches in India to disciple and train more than 2 million believers.

Pr Fomum also considered fasting as one of the weapons of Christian Spiritual Warfare. He carried out over 250 fasts ranging from three days to forty days, drinking only water or water supplemented with soluble vitamins. Called by the Lord to a distinct ministry of intercession, he pioneered fasting and prayer movements and led in battles against principalities and powers obstructing the progress of the Gospel and God's global purposes. He was enabled to carry out 3 supra – long fasts of between 52 and 70 days in his final years.

Pr Fomum chose a lifestyle of simplicity and "self- imposed poverty" in order to invest more funds into the critical work of evangelism, soul winning, church-planting and the building up of believers. Knowing the importance of money and its role in the battle to reach those without Christ with the glorious Gospel, he and his wife grew to investing 92.5% of their earned income from all sources (salaries, allowances, royalties and cash gifts) into the Gospel. They invested with the hope that, as they grew in the knowledge and the love of the Lord, and the perishing souls of people, they would one day invest 99% of their income into the Gospel.

He was married to Prisca Zei Fomum and they had seven children who are all involved in the work of the Gospel, some serving as missionaries. Prisca is a national and international minister, specializing in the winning and discipling of children to Jesus Christ. She also communicates and imparts the vision of ministry to children with a view to raising and building up ministers to them.

The Professor owed all that he was and all that God had done through him, to the unmerited favour and blessing of God and to his worldwide army of friends and co-workers. He considered himself nothing without them and the blessing of God; and would have amounted to nothing but for them. All praise and glory to Jesus Christ!

facebook.com/cmfionline

twitter.com/cmfionline

instagram.com/cmfionline

pinterest.com/cmfionline

youtube.com/cmfionline

ALSO BY Z.T. FOMUM

https://ztfbooks.com

THE CHRISTIAN WAY

1. The Way Of Life
2. The Way Of Obedience
3. The Way Of Discipleship
4. The Way Of Sanctification
5. The Way Of Christian Character
6. The Way Of Spiritual Power
7. The Way Of Christian Service
8. The Way Of Spiritual Warfare
9. The Way Of Suffering For Christ
10. The Way Of Victorious Praying
11. The Way Of Overcomers
12. The Way Of Spiritual Encouragement
13. The Way Of Loving The Lord

THE PRAYER POWER SERIES

1. The Way Of Victorious Praying
2. The Ministry Of Fasting
3. The Art Of Intercession
4. The Practice Of Intercession
5. Praying With Power
6. Practical Spiritual Warfare Through Prayer
7. Moving God Through Prayer
8. The Ministry Of Praise And Thanksgiving
9. Waiting On The Lord In Prayer

PRACTICAL HELPS FOR OVERCOMERS

LEADING GOD'S PEOPLE

PRACTICAL HELPS IN SANCTIFICATION

MAKING SPIRITUAL PROGRESS

3. Making Spiritual Progress, Volume 1
4. Making Spiritual Progress, Volume 2
5. Making Spiritual Progress, Volume 3
6. Making Spiritual Progress, Volume 4
7. Moving on With The Lord Jesus Christ
8. The Narrow Way (Volume 1)
9. Making Spiritual Progress (Volumes 1-4)

EVANGELISM

1. 36 Reasons For Winning The Lost To Christ
2. Soul Winning, Volume 1
3. Soul Winning, Volume 2
4. The Winning of The Lost as Life's Supreme Task
5. Salvation And Soul-Winning
6. Soul Winning And The Making Of Disciples
7. <u>Victorious Soul-Winning</u>

GOD LOVES YOU

1. God's Love And Forgiveness
2. The Way Of Life
3. Come Back Home My Son; I Still Love You
4. Jesus Loves You And Wants To Heal You
5. Come And See; Jesus Has Not Changed!
6. Celebrity A Mask
7. Encounter The Saviour
8. Meet The Liberator
9. Jesus Saves And Heals Today
10. Jesus is The Answer

OTHER BOOKS

1. The Missionary as a Son
2. What Our Ministry is
3. Conserver la Moisson
4. Disciples of Jesus Christ to Make Disciples For Jesus Christ
5. The House Church in God's Eternal Purposes
6. Christian Maturation
7. Heroes of the Kingdom
8. Spiritual Leadership in the Pattern of Gideon
9. The School of Evangelism
10. A Good Minister of Jesus Christ
11. Building a Spiritual Nation: The Foundation
12. Building a Spiritual Nation: Spiritual Statesmanship
13. Removing Obstacles Through Prayer and Fasting
14. The Chronicles of Our Ministry
15. The Making of Disciples: The Master's Way

DISTRIBUTORS OF ZTF BOOKS

These books can be obtained in French and English Language from any of the following distribution outlets:

EDITIONS DU LIVRE CHRETIEN (ELC)

- **Location:** Paris, France
- **Email:** editionlivrechretien@gmail.com
- **Phone:** +33 6 98 00 90 47

INTERNET

- **Location:** on all major online **eBook, Audiobook** and **print-on-demand** (paperback) retailers (Amazon, Google, iBooks, B&N, Ingram, NotionPress, etc.).
- **Email**: ztfbooks@cmfionline.org
- **Phone**: +47 454 12 804
- **Website**: ztfbooks.com

CPH YAOUNDE

- **Location:** Yaounde, Cameroon
- **Email:** editionsztf@gmail.com
- **Phone:** +237 74756559

ZTF LITERATURE AND MEDIA HOUSE

- **Location:** Lagos, Nigeria
- **Email:** zlmh@ztfministry.org
- **Phone:** +2348152163063

CPH BURUNDI

- **Location:** Bujumbura, Burundi
- **Email:** cph-burundi@ztfministry.org
- **Phone:** +257 79 97 72 75

CPH UGANDA

- **Location:** Kampala, Uganda
- **Email:** cph-uganda@ztfministry.org
- **Phone:** +256 785 619613

CPH SOUTH AFRICA

- **Location:** Johannesburg, RSA
- **Email:** tantohtantoh@yahoo.com
- **Phone:** +27 83 744 5682

www.ingramcontent.com/pod-product-compliance
Lightning Source LLC
Chambersburg PA
CBHW031500130726
47989CB00003B/1482